P9-CSB-798

For our ferocious kitten, Bonnie Bow —B.H.

Text copyright © 2019 by Bridget Heos
Illustrations copyright © 2019 by David Clark

All rights reserved. For information about permission to reproduce selections from this book,
write to trade.permissions@hmco.com or to Permissions, Houghton Mifflin Harcourt Publishing Company,
3 Park Avenue, 19th Floor, New York, New York 10016.

hmhco.com

The illustrations in this book were done in pen and ink, watercolor, and digital media.

The text type was set in Agenda and Felt-Tip Woman.
The display type was hand-lettered by David Clark.

Library of Congress Cataloging-in-Publication Data
Names: Heos, Bridget, author. | Clark, David, 1960 March 19– illustrator.
Title: Just like us!, cats / by Bridget Heos ; illustrated by David Clark.
Other titles: Cats
Description: Boston ; New York : Houghton Mifflin Harcourt, 2018. | Audience:
Ages 4–7. | Audience: K to grade 3. | Includes bibliographical references
and index.
Identifiers: LCCN 2017043229 | ISBN 9781328791849
Subjects: LCSH: Felidae—Juvenile literature. | CYAC: Cat family (Mammals).
Classification: LCC QL737.C23 H4576 2018 | DDC 599.75—dc23
LC record available at https://lccn.loc.gov/2017043229

ISBN: 978-0-358-00389-2 (paperback)

Printed in Malaysia
TWP 10 9 8 7 6 5 4 3 2 1
4500735403

Lexile Level	Guided Reading	Fountas & Pinnell	Interest Level
850L	T	R	Grade 2–6

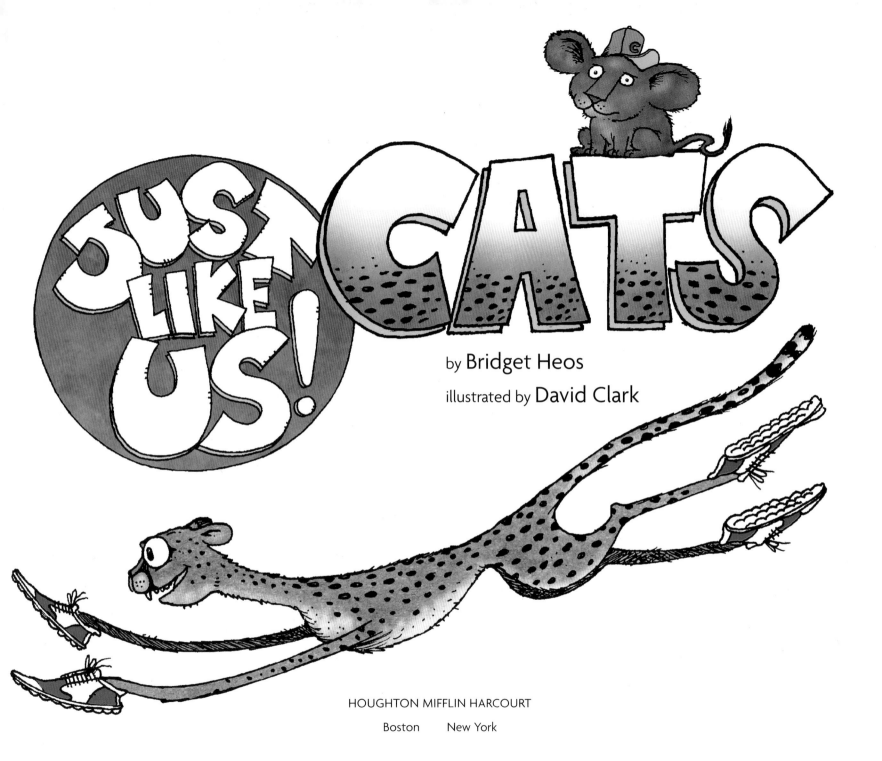

JUST LIKE US! CATS

by Bridget Heos

illustrated by David Clark

HOUGHTON MIFFLIN HARCOURT

Boston   New York

CATS

The Inside Scoop

CATS HAVE RETRACTABLE CLAWS, razor-sharp teeth, and tails for balancing. Humans don't. But in some ways, cats and people are alike. Cats are loving parents and great diplomats, but they also wage war against each other, just as we do. Like humans, cats can live in almost any environment, but for some, there's no place like our homes. Domestic cats settled down alongside people around 10,000 years ago and have been our cozy companions ever since. Read on to learn how cats—both wild and mild—really are . . . just like us.

SNOW GEAR

THE FIRST CATS evolved in Asia. From there, they migrated throughout the world, just as people have. We rely on creativity for survival, inventing things such as needles and thread to sew warm coats. Cats are born ready. The Canada lynx has a coat so dense that heat escapes only through its eyes and ears. Subzero temperatures feel like a balmy day to the lynx, and it actually gets hot while hunting its favorite meal—the snowshoe hare!

And though we rely on snowshoes, the lynx's big round paws let it trot atop the snow's frozen crust. Unfortunately for the lynx, the snowshoe hare has adapted the same trait to escape the wily predator. And so the two play an ongoing game of cat and mouse, or in this case, cat and hare.

On the Road Again...

Cats take the easiest routes through their territories, trotting along trails, roads, or, in the case of Siberian tigers, frozen rivers. Humans have long traveled across ice to avoid slow trudges through snow. Tigers trot atop ice for the same reason. Unlike the Canada lynx, whose snowshoe-like paws keep its light body atop the snow, the heavy tiger would fall through no matter how big its paws. So it takes the path of least resistance, albeit an icy one!

CAT FIGHT!

CATS MAY BE the world's most effective carnivores, but they face tough competition from other cats. Just as humans do, cats defend their territories while ruthlessly conquering other lands. It begins when cubs grow up and leave their mother's side. Daughters settle near their mothers. But sons wander through other cats' territories until they are ready to stake their claim and mate. Then the battle begins. The invading males fight the defending males—sometimes to the death!

Female cats won't mate when they are still caring for their young. So if the overthrower wins, it sets out to do the unthinkable: kill the cubs. Mothers fiercely protect their cubs, though, sometimes killing the overthrower. Another cat may have started the fight, but Mama finishes it.

DIPLOCATS

ON THE OTHER HAND, cats can be quite diplomatic. To avoid conflict, they leave each other messages. A puma scrapes the ground with its hind legs, creating a heap of dirt. Then it pees on the mound. The mound serves as the message notification. The message itself is in the urine. It tells whether the cat is male or female, neighbor or stranger. A neighbor is nothing to worry about; cats are friendly with, and often related to, those that live nearby. But a stranger may be looking for a fight. For a peaceful outcome, avoidance is best. The puma checks the freshness of the urine scent. A marking several days old indicates the coast is clear. If the scent is fresh, however, it's best to move on. Be and let be, as the saying goes, or in this case, pee and let pee.

Cats rule! Dogs drool? Dogs live and hunt in packs, which would seem an advantage over the more solitary cat. Not so! When the first cat species arrived in America by crossing a land bridge, they hunted more effectively than many of the resident dogs. This, in turn, may have led to the extinction of forty canine species. In other words, among carnivores, the top dog is actually the cat.

UNEASY LIES THE HEAD

OF ALL CATS, lions are the most social. They live in family groups called prides. Mothers, daughters, aunts, and female cousins reside in the same kingdom for generations. A small number of "lion kings" protect the pride and father the cubs. But their reign is only temporary. They are constantly challenged by outsiders and are eventually overthrown.

The game of capture the crown begins at age two, when young males are banished from the pride by their father. The brothers and cousins form a coalition of their own, traveling together through enemy territory. If caught trespassing, they will be killed. Those that survive, however, soon challenge other lion kings for their territory. If the old kings lose the fight, they must flee or be killed. The victors roar loudly, signaling for miles around that they are the new kings. But not for long. In a few years, they too will fall from power.

LION QUEENS

WHEN THEY'RE NOT KILLING each other, lions get along great! The lionesses do most of the hunting. When working together, they surround the prey. One lion gives chase, and another captures and kills the animal as it tries to flee. Then it's suppertime. The male lions often insist on eating first, even though the females made the kill. But eventually all join in, including cubs that aren't old enough to hunt and elderly lions that no longer can.

MEOW, QUIT IT!

CATS ARE SUCH EFFICIENT HUNTERS that they have plenty of downtime. In fact, they've been known to sleep up to twenty hours a day! Well, that's what the grownups do. Like human kids, cubs and kittens think naptime is boring. (Babies of big cats are cubs; those of small cats are kittens.) They want to play, play, play! Their favorite game is wrestling, and the matches sometimes take place right on top of their sleeping mother. The adults are quite patient with the kittens and may join in for a minute or two. The play serves a purpose after all. Wrestling strengthens the kittens so that they'll be ready to hunt. Play today, slay tomorrow!

DEN MOTHER

MOST MAMA CATS raise their cubs alone. The Pallas's cat lives in the mountains. In the summer, the mother makes a den in the crevices of rocks. When it gets cold, she moves her kittens to a snuggly marmot burrow underground. At first, she nuzzles them constantly and feeds them milk. But soon it's time to go back to work. After all, somebody has to bring home the bacon, or in this case, the pika.

Cat-toos. Camouflage keeps cats hidden from their prey. Spotted cats blend in with the dappled shade of the rainforest. Beige lions fade into the dry grass of the savanna. And underneath it all, a cat's skin matches the markings of its fur. Unlike fur patterns, these skin markings have no real purpose, because in the wild, cats have fur. Only certain domestic cats have been bred to be hairless, and they don't need to hide from their food. Kibble can't run away!

KITTENGARTEN

MEALTIME IS SCHOOL TIME for the kittens. The first lesson is simple: Mom drags a pika back to the den and eats it. The cubs take note: Mom eats pikas. Pikas must be yummy. Got it! Next, Mom encourages the kittens to eat some pika themselves. Then, for a more paws-on lesson, Mom brings back a live but wounded pika. The cubs are reluctant at first, but eventually they pounce. It's the cubs' homework assignment after all. Mom's not going to do it for them.

Pika
101

TAKE YOUR CUBS TO HUNT DAY

FINALLY, AT SIX WEEKS, it's time for some on-the-job training. The cubs follow their mom on the hunt. If there's danger, she growls and they hide. Multitasking is never easy. Often, with cubs by Mom's side, the hunt goes awry. But the cubs must learn to hunt, as their survival will depend on it. Over time the cubs grow more adventurous and wander farther to practice hunting. Their mother calls them closer with a "yow." And it's no use pretending they can't hear it; the sound carries for a mile.

WORLD CLASS CAT-HLETES

IN THE EARLY DAYS OF HUNTING, humans had only knives for weapons. Our prey—antelope, gazelles, and wildebeests—were faster than any person. But we had an ace up our sleeves: we could run until our prey got tired. Then it could be killed. Cats are great runners too. But for them, life is not a marathon but a sprint. The cheetah's lean, muscular body is built for speed, while its paws are a cross between high-performance tires and track cleats. Claws provide push-off for building speed, and treads prevent slippage on turns. Reaching speeds of sixty-four miles per hour (104 kph), the cheetah easily outsprints its prey. The cheetah is twice as fast as a human sprinter, but a distance runner would leave the cat in the dust. In fact, top marathon runners can outpace most land animals—especially in warm conditions.

People rely on tools for hunting and gathering. Cats have tools too—built in, of course! Their retractable claws remain tucked inside the paws while the cat stalks (so that the clickety-clack doesn't alert prey). When it's time to pounce, the claws shoot out like switchblades. Muscles at the base of the whiskers allow them to reach forward, feeling for the prey's neck. The cat's teeth prove to be its deadliest weapon of all. The bite, as devastating as it is accurate, paralyzes or immediately kills the prey. Cats also have flashlights built into their eyes—an essential adaptation for night hunters. Mirrorlike structures at the backs of the eyes capture light and reflect it back on the prey. But cats are far-sighted. Even well-lit objects appear blurry up close. Whiskers are the cat version of reading glasses.

You're Finished
Line

A PERFECT TEN!

THE ANCESTORS OF ALL CATS lived in trees. But many species, including lions and tigers, now reside at ground level and climb only with difficulty. Even agile housecats, though they can climb up a tree easily, struggle to get down (and need the occasional rescue). The margay, on the other hand, is the gymnast of the cat world. It can climb down a tree headfirst, leap from branch to branch, and even hang upside down by its feet. When walking a tightrope-like branch, it uses its tail as a balancing pole. To walk down a tree trunk, it rotates its ankles more than 180 degrees. This would be like a gymnast turning her feet completely backwards!

Monkeying Around Margays eat tamarin monkeys. To lure them closer, the cat imitates the sounds of baby tamarins. But the margay isn't a very good actor. Hearing what only sort of sounds like a baby, the tamarin parents approach with caution and flee when they see the sound's true source. Still, margay mothers teach their kittens to make the tamarin noises. Perhaps more acting lessons would help?

CATS HAVE ANOTHER athletic trait: power. A leopard can tackle animals more than ten times its size, so impalas, elands, and even young giraffes are on the menu. A cat's eyes are bigger than its stomach, though. Many cats bury their leftovers in the snow—the feline version of the deep freezer. Others store them in a quiet stream. But the powerful leopard puts its groceries away in the highest cupboard, hauling it up a tree and laying it on a branch! That keeps it safe from poor climbers, such as lions. Or so the leopard thinks. With a tasty treat literally dangling over the lion's head, it will sometimes scale the tree, however awkwardly. And there go the leftovers!

SUGAR-FREE DIET

CATS ARE "SUGAR BLIND." They lack the gene that allows other mammals to taste sweetness. This explains why housecats show scant interest in people food, whereas dogs have never met a leftover they didn't like. Cats may turn down the dessert menu, but they really, really like the main course. An adult tiger will eat one-fifth of its weight, or a hundred pounds (45 kg) of meat, in a single meal! That would be like a one-hundred-pound kid eating a twenty-pound steak. You might say that instead of a sweet tooth, cats have a meat tooth!

GETTING ALONG SWIMMINGLY

DESPITE THEIR REPUTATION for hating water, some types of cats are great swimmers . . . just like us! Top human divers can hold their breath for more than twenty minutes. Likewise, jaguars can stay underwater for several minutes while hunting for caimans and capybaras in South American rivers. They are good distance swimmers, too, using their webbed feet to paddle across rivers a mile (2 km) wide. Tigers and fishing cats take to the water for fun and food as well. For all their swimming prowess, cats' choice of stroke may be surprising. They do the doggy paddle!

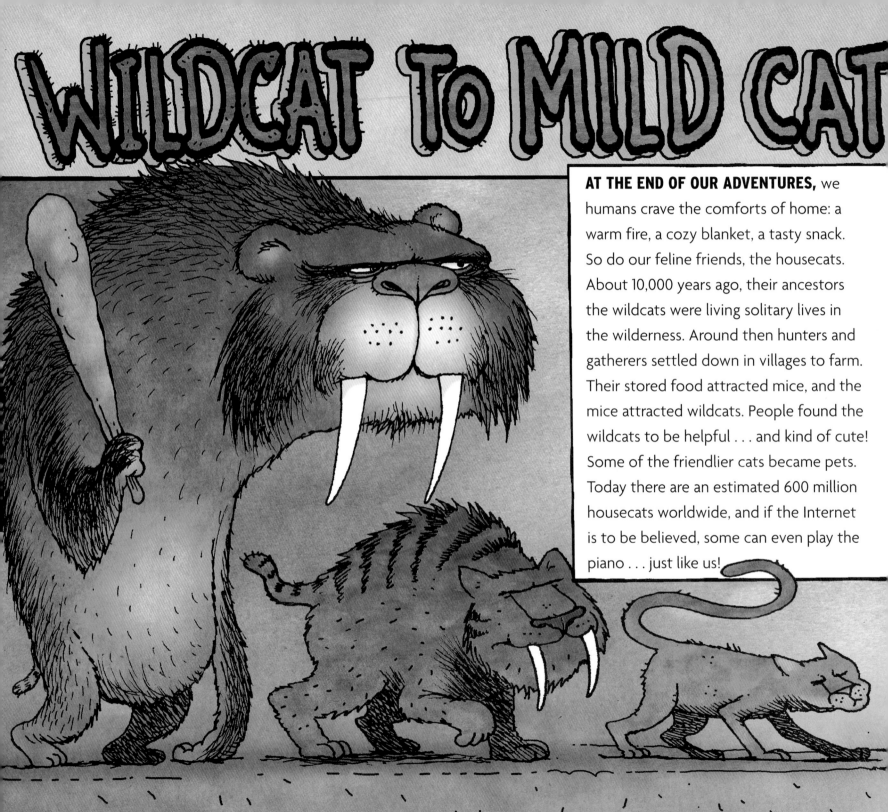

WILDCAT TO MILD CAT

AT THE END OF OUR ADVENTURES, we humans crave the comforts of home: a warm fire, a cozy blanket, a tasty snack. So do our feline friends, the housecats. About 10,000 years ago, their ancestors the wildcats were living solitary lives in the wilderness. Around then hunters and gatherers settled down in villages to farm. Their stored food attracted mice, and the mice attracted wildcats. People found the wildcats to be helpful . . . and kind of cute! Some of the friendlier cats became pets. Today there are an estimated 600 million housecats worldwide, and if the Internet is to be believed, some can even play the piano . . . just like us!

SAY WHAT?

adaptation a characteristic, physical or behavioral, that helps members of a species to survive.

camouflage a pattern that blends in with the surroundings.

carnivore an animal that mainly eats meat; also an order of mammals that includes dogs, cats, bears, and others.

coalition a group that works together toward a common goal.

cub the young of many carnivores, including large cats.

den an animal home, often used as a safe shelter for the young.

dense having parts of the whole (such as hairs of a coat) tightly packed together.

evolve to change gradually over time as helpful mutations are passed from generation to generation.

extinction the dying off of all animals in a species.

housecat a species of cat that was domesticated from the wildcat.

kitten the young offspring of a small cat.

migrate to seek food and shelter in a new region, seasonally or permanently.

pride a family of lions.

retractable claws sharp nails that are sheathed inside the paws when muscles and tendons are relaxed, but protrude when they tighten.

territory an area inhabited by a specific animal or animals.

trait a characteristic that is passed from parent to child.

BIBLIOGRAPHY

Alderton, David. *Wild Cats of the World*. New York: Facts on File, 1993.

Bhattacharya, Shaoni. "New Cat Family Tree Tracks Global Feline Success." *New Scientist*. January 6, 2006. (www.newscientist.com/article/dn8545-new-cat-family-tree-tracks-global-feline-success)

Biello, David. "Strange but True: Cats Cannot Taste Sweets." *Scientific American*. August 16, 2007. (www.scientificamerican.com/article/strange-but-true-cats-cannot-taste-sweets)

Bryna, Jeanna. "Usain Bolt vs. the Cheetah: Olympians of the Animal Kingdom." Live Science. July 30, 2012. (www.livescience.com/21944-usain-bolt-vs-cheetah-animal-olympics.html)

Defenders of Wildlife. "Canada Lynx." (www.defenders.org/canada-lynx/basic-facts; accessed January 3, 2017)

Hunter, Luke. *Wild Cats of the World*. London: Bloomsbury, 2015.

Kitchener, Andrew. *The Natural History of the Wild Cats*. Ithaca, NY: Cornell University Press, 1991.

Lehnert, Erin. "Cheetah." Animal Diversity Web. (animaldiversity.org/accounts/Acinonyx_jubatus; accessed January 4, 2017)

Main, Douglas. "Becoming King: Why So Few Male Lions Survive to Adulthood." Live Science. November 27, 2013. (www.livescience.com/41572-male-lion-survival.html)

Mamon, Anwar, dir. "The Story of Cats: Asia to Africa," Part 1. *Nature*. PBS. Aired November 2, 2016.

Mamon, Anwar, dir. "The Story of Cats: Into the Americas," Part 2. *Nature*. PBS. Aired November 9, 2016.

Quammen, David. "The Short Happy Life of a Serengeti Lion." *National Geographic*. August 2013. (ngm.nationalgeographic.com/print/2013/08/serengeti-lions/quammen-text)

Slaght, Jonathan. "East of Siberia: Walking Rivers with Tigers." *Scientific American*. May 11, 2016. (blogs.scientificamerican.com/guest-blog/east-of-siberia-walking-rivers-with-tigers)

Sunquist, Fiona, and Mel Sunquist. *The Wild Cat Book*. Chicago: University of Chicago Press, 2014.

Thompson, Tanja. "Competition from the Ancestors of Cats Drove the Extinction of Many Species of Ancient Dogs." University of Gothenburg. July 14, 2015. (www.gu.se/english/about_the_university/news-calendar/News_detail/competition-from-the-ancestors-of-cats-drove-the-extinction-of-many-species-of-ancient-dogs.cid1313224)

BRIDGET HEOS is the author of more than sixty nonfiction titles for kids and teens, including *Shell, Beak, Tusk; Stronger Than Steel; It's Getting Hot in Here; I, Fly;* and *What to Expect When You're Expecting Larvae.* She's also the author of the picture books *Mustache Baby* and *Mustache Baby Meets His Match.* Bridget lives in Kansas City with her husband and four children, and you can learn more about her and her books at authorbridgetheos.com.

DAVID CLARK has illustrated numerous picture books, including *Pirate Bob, Fractions in Disguise,* and *The Mine-o-Saur.* He also co-created—and illustrates—the nationally syndicated comic strip *Barney & Clyde.* David lives in Virginia with his family, and you can learn more about his books and his comics at sites.google.com/site/davidclark1988.

Photo Credits: Linda Freshwaters Arndt: 7 • Sean Crane: 24 • Fanie and Annette Heymans: 9 • Michael Lane: 22, cover • Paul McKenzie: 13, 19, cover • Etienne Oosthuizen: 4, 15, cover • Octavio Campos Salles: 21 • Sergey Taran: 17 • Max Waugh: 10 • Andrew Whittaker: 27 • Burnell Yow!: 29, cover